Dog Day Economy

Dog Day Economy

Ted Rees

ROOF BOOKS
NEW YORK

ISBN: 978-1-7379703-2-3
Library of Congress Control Number: 2021952800

This book is dedicated to the memory of Sid Sobel,
and to those who have disappeared.

As ever, this book is for Theo and Canela,
and yes, you too, Wiz.

NEW YORK | Council on   This book is made possible by the New York State
STATE OF OPPORTUNITY. | the Arts   Council on the Arts with the support of the Office of
the Governor and the New York State Legislature.

Roof Books
are published by
Segue Foundation
300 Bowery, New York, NY 10012
seguefoundation.com

Roof Books
are distributed by
Small Press Distribution
1341 Seventh Street
Berkeley, CA. 94710-1403
800-869-7553 or spdbooks.org

Contents

Economy, a Reshaped Spit   7

Dog Day Scrolls   73

    I: Dog   74

    II: Day   88

    III: Scrolls   113

    Notes & Acknowledgements   135

handwritten note left
in the unremarkable room
where we burned our papers
and set off the alarm.
A crowd gathers
on a strip of grass.

Economy, a Reshaped Spit

It is not enough to be sick in halves;
a man's gotta go the whole hog.

—Dambudzo Marechera

Traced to forgiveness,
where ways deep as pasture
wand rich cell phone video
with sexual porridge
across the midwest.

Depressing couple of years flavoring
a damaged box of Franzia,
efficient peril moving alleged mountains,
their crisis just accent to the real.

Our spectacles reflect this terrarium
of failure plinthed, affectively disordered,
slowly in the branches rumbling
self as a deepening of blood
setting into sofa fabric,
cancelled carpet daddy yum,
a bus can count him
ping-ponging angles blubber
grainy footage
banter this global position
thrown to the waves.

He finds himself on a frame slack blue
thus redoubtable in its smudgy shriek,
come and knock on our door
who, beyond the structureless
salmon shorts of our despondence,
remains callous, in uproar, age of 26.

The wrong people approach the rifle.
I love a man in traffic,
men in traffic, tense
in the clovers.

Of apparent interest at least,
matrix of skin sure beltline
thread-holding the formula,
oh you reach your hand up to your next
icky somatic guarantee:

lark of a neon slouch
lark incomprehensibly stable
it hailed an hour ago,
forethoughts' supple flesh ellipsis
dragging a suitcase stuffed with specimen jars
and co-ordinates of the best rib shacks
in the panhandle,
leaping porno flask
passed around post-pew
a floppy torque of old Babylon
and hogs destroying all evidences,
wade in the pond.

Life were cheap candles in fog
the elegance of that genre—
scratched lens and spit perforations directing
no and no this greasy strip
and massaged water stains.

The problem, he was saying,
is chuck banderole slobber,
aren't any papers in this
our daily hibernation's colours.

The problem was last seen
everywhere the problem was,
too inward to ever float,
whiskers in a minor key drone more
like a wail or a keen.
We're edges, comme ci comme ca ja.

Later that morning, the problem
was runny eggs or the morning itself.
I tug at my left nipple
reading Notley by candlelight in a van screw work,
nuzzled burden of verse—
there is no romance mowing the lawn
the problem was the lawn.
Could not recognize the faces standing over me.
Did you sing your chomps
into your fragmentary subjecthood
or did you unmute the problem
witnessed by a neighbour,
the apparition that is melody
tool demonstr sin city dairies theuboomf inspctqn
we misremember words we summon
a directory of murmuring alleys
all our harms like weaverbirds.

For me suddenly the roar
wined on the dawn killing of
the motor age bankruptcy
witnessed in a shed complex adjacent
best known for (blank) and fishing for
business therefore engineered
a distraction leather-clad
women gyrate in cages behind the lobby

Imagine directing assistants
placing a painting of smacking lips
above the master bed
in the Zurich pied-a-terre while your advisor says,
The zeitgeist has lost touch with the data.
His mouth's corners host a foamy buildup.
I got fucked in a basement bathroom
by some sinecuring fop from Dubai.

Use this text to sell bottle service
and expired film, plague,
signifieds never surfaces is a demand, dammit
light, dammit graceful light named empire,
shrill blue fields and fields stubborn, yellowing.
I king urinal and expanding void
whereas that's my sleep mantra,
rapids in a canoe lulling route
to obscurity's portage, a better way
to say frozen ground at dawn
or an epidemic builds
wherein we need to spend hours in the woodshed,
emerging only to pour hot diarrea
on our careers, ensuring
that a would-be ladder's a sawed toon,
really just hokum clobber prescription.

I've shut myself off to light
except from impulse.
My friend said they done close
and I was hard the day's remainder,
locked roll gates slam, slam, slam. We threw
ourselves in a pile across the trolley tracks:
viscid, viscid, viscid yoking skin
outpost of self in ecstasy in retirement,
the companies stretch
yawn
check for flesh between teeth.
A CD skipping *it is painful*
past twenty years' metonym.

So we image ourselves in our persistence,
a skin fragment inhaled
after turning to dust?
You see here the American home,
brackish tanninated tides lap,
we're all sitting in it
we all scream while asleep.

He sighs, "Most of
our galactic family of light for assistance
has never arrived," and slips back in
to his wet clothes waiting
for a dryer.

Who knew him felt that ochre cast lethal thrum
fostering rankled substrate trench feelings
poured concrete, sod, institution brand cedar mulch.

Go to where the Ikeas are,
spritz acid in the meatballs,
purchase miniature plastic palm
skiffle to the next destination:
thick stands of ditches and untended woods
heaved as a party intermittent the western creases.

Then it goes circular back to the pit
sometimes filled with rain
where's not a grid though
thought by anyone the game
of tag's associative spindle
haphazard in its riggings

a conversation re: remotenesses
unseen hollow in the face prison
to expect to be tempted
and also stillness lost.

Once declaimed an ode to a
intoxicated witness,
considered the valley in mud
after being prompted.

Echoes in patches removed,
packed in boxes
willingly, citing these terrors.

Partially undressed and crying,
I didn't feel like talking.
The firm walls surfaced.

Guns have slipped back into holsters
and diplomats behind their desks,
leather fingers along leather
joy chamber scorching dangit,
it was God or a transformer exploding
just the initial stage peeking around corners
smiling Goofy voice repeated yelling
a single pop from below
pallets greasy with pheromones
reliable sources mossy or flexing
in sunlight VANDAL COWARD
INFORM RAT!

This mason jar of liquid LSD
waylaid in the hills
is one of the few slinks toward measure
of the hearts yet a fool scrapples
the whole deal. It's this damn country.
Left at first fork, drag your peepers
ubiquitous as this cresting wind
FIVE VERBAL ASSAULTS
AGAINST FAMILY & FRIENDS
we are ever reliant on
the nocturnal luminosity of information
and its failures, yea the shimmy
of the clutch forever blowing abject
bubbles stored as thoughts at cellar rear.

To the ebb it's wild
theses backstroke through rummy
of consumer choice,
winter fashion execution

grey referent making me wet
out the train window is the flair and mistake
of the season on the nod
bony lady stole his short
stuck it in toothless mouth
Your apprehension draws an image
beati qui lugent et cetera
it is a sensing toward sangfroid
and flow of loanwords,
cruel wind at our dumpers.

Balloons fell, glasses clinked,
street protests levelled a city
bang head for reverie or present
a tempting set of stropped
banter relationals imitative
of Coromandel screens,
shall I finger my scars more?
Do you hear the faucet of meaning?
The all-region DVD player quit its spin
and the monitor blued, we bounced.

Smirk, slurping justice
formless interior
the party that has been in the backyard the whole time
secret recipes for tatertot hotdish
blood Satan Satan not otherwise on ice.

You can't beg for better words
thawing, disintegrating underfoot
yon silence of drawing.
What happened to plumbago
but sheen snapped
for materials reach outward
first: we drop buttonwood twigs
off one side of the bridge,
a shore hence recollection:
a gasp or serrefine
lead-up to yet more dismal bog.

That is a doomed campaign
for a more rigid flocked surface
of temporal concerns,
gagged undulation in the shanty
we strip and ablute each eventide,
good news is bad news:
we've breath, rawdogged
in a castle dungeon,
dunked myself in a barrel
of lube, a political theatre regurgitation
where hallways are charred,
long and damp, bootprints
on low-pile carpet.

He would sniff Ajax just to feel the burn
asynchronous to my youth in ditches
the grey matter of free will crunching
its way through the forest of worship
shame of clashing melodic intervals
self on screen not always so synced
but fun for a while 'til a fanatic walked,
they all walk.

It's why our scrambled intention to learn
how to trache the horizon was initiated.
Sadly, its execution was tragicomic,
deeply compressed yet histrionic, accurate yet
subject to the whims of the board
on which we all opened fire. Damn Ambien,
fucked five ways to Friday keep it down down,
landed into a house that ain't mine,
baton gauntlet psychic scan
and where are my contours, my slop?

Did you reel in the sandtrap rubbing slammed
against illusive green?

"I pissed on roses and an African tortoise
roaming the grounds," he says
of bridges soar his corneas,
heap, heap on excesses and surely the soul
or another drastic image will flutter
into that overturn grabbing the throat,
thumbs at center a loading dock for sex crimes
amidst other conveyances of slavery
it's what the border is for:
an unyielding romance void
and dustborne illness fabricator.

She calls it knife salsa.
Until then, bleached remains.

Right now, it looks like substance flashing
from a malfunctioning squeeze bottle
slipping on orange spooge, forgotten veins,
sick and wearing unlaced Tims.
Huffing gas, staging a coup on the bunny hill,
attempt after attempt to avoid catastrophe in the glade.

Like things cocooned in sweat seeking the river people,
bad camp burning near the tracks they say.
If so, it will be yet more proof that the hugs don't work:
curses on his arms, admonitions from Hollywood
sleeping it off in the tub, the deepening suicide of July,
dust collecting on serape, what seems evident
is pretending the meals are going well
or finding maps back to the cistern,
another breath method. Quick and shallow
isn't easy, it's questions of closets in warfare.

Looking sexed-up from one angle
on the situation, correspondence with manic scorch
eyeballs and lightening curtain.

Bonking moss and jet engine missives constant
little tautological buds' year-round blooms
in the middle path resembling death but is its antipode, just
rural and socked with fog in March, on dispersive being
people flail.

How does this circuit
have an interpretive value and what mineral dyes
the collection ponds that vivid?

Alternatively, we could inquire about pods at the podport,
smother ourselves in frictionless language like it was shit:
areas that read as exploded hillocks or desolate malls almost
forgot the sirens, the plunge
into what resolves in a scream:
no faceless no, creamy beige smudges that's vista
is the forensic file on the Chupa Chup on my lips.
Poor substitute we agree
that a shoreline's developing.

Into the rapid arpeggiations
trapped in breeze

necrotic flesh
the hound digs and digs

fate across water
gray reflection porous

what was the flavor
ash and limes

pretty good business cautioned
pretty good business

flipped our fartsacks under that arbor
like a box airing up

and he's waggling his number
out the door frigid ideation

shaggy and waxing
mistake of our plane

victorious on the lists
busted kneecap capiche

dipped in soda
and flirty with a comb.

Once you get the wound
there are other changes.
Like the inadequacy

of the modular,
our rousting yet we can not get out.

Dear incursion on value relations:
your name is Glenn and you're deep
in a political thicket in a mid-Atlantic state
limned with toll roads, sandy loam.
You will resign.
My jaw will slope ever more drastic
gnaw of night.

Wrung tears, wet bread,
pigeons in the eaves,
they have their faces in data, they're us
at the community bulletin board renaissance.
We practice our letters
and never stop bopping solo,
lovely curvature
to which theatrical distances yield.

My face and roads right, muffled Sunday
staunch and stew-like, able
to get access because it is pervasive,
thin yet unyielding.

The smile occasionally accompanies the fall,
conservatively, half the time, and thus
we find ourselves active sissies wall-to-wall
smooched yellow sofa, we sing
of kitchen tile and plunge our fists
into police scanners.
Strop me, get it, all the bases.
And the mound. What's the use
of all Americans, of stripling
metaphor, dander and the piled
curtains.

Foul trouble
through a courtyard with peeling paint,
the exception
relied more and more
on consuming the age of
the suffering it embodied.

Boomlet in hell.
A blue blazer,
human scalp,
cropland thicker,
a shadow sex recurring.
Confirmed buzz
as well as terrestrial animals
likely to weaken.

In plots regaled by flippant vandals
any sparrow sings then halts as you approach.
What of sloppy tubes running, rearing their legs
given what some call the past, a diurnal memorial
wearing a brick smock, thus in appearance:
year of the stripped screw,
one jagged finger
in the pail catching roof water,
six subject titles of ongoing threads.
Less an inch from my damn face
is air or a reasonable alternative.
I would love a bite of your lava cake
afflicted as I am by ongoing cycles of spew
and cool in sun.

When his son said the cave, 'twas a bevy
of single-panel jokes and *soma contra ptoma*,
refs bammed times two despite my affections
she was insistent on gazing north
in a daisy-yellow dress that swept the dust
a blanket held slack at her side— accustomed,
we recall with ease the archive but nude, lying
as it does in its pocked misanthrope
and golden dependence. Would it heaved
itself beyond the boulders amidst hi-frequency buzz,
another cursed dream, another blanket or system of such
found in brush and poison oak next a cur
partially under rotted stump, fur clinging to stripped bone,
collar loose the hollow neck.

Since clingfilm's déclassé, we had to search for a novel
textile that wrapped itself in what was
coming like piffs of fungal spores
shovels in fresh clay
the flimsy narrative of the tents,
what a shrug to power signifying its grim persistence
ending in a reefer and some guys checking something out on
   the roof.
The party line is rags left behind in grey matter:
has me thinkin' 'bout dinner,
got packets of Bernard championed
by no one, elbow cradling head against slab bench
like traditional love, directionless and punitive,
such membrane of families
gushy peepers in the morn.

Appointment in a remote town,
its winds reportedly artworks whipped
with a sense of industry.

Following this article, straddle
the fault emailed from a conversation
that blood evidence, as well as animal feed,
learned its wettest tense.

Demands of so-called rationality buckling
chainlink, a frilly new means of extending ourselves
to questions ranging from barking to sly fleur-de-lys
spraypainted on the Tuff Shed.

The sky is changing and the mortar thins:
these are lessons qua saltines with government jam
and the gallery fills with smoke of hypersonic trance
that runs things, a plot that ends in a cardboard box
   generation
and paranoid circle rituals.

For clarity's sake, I am at home but done with all that,
shorn temple bathed in sin and lesser missiles,
loafing for a loaf.

And when kinship spikes you in the arm,
there are no musical numbers to distract from
   immediacy's mush.

You eat the mush
and finger nearby relics of your symbolic order squealing
in peatlands, thus ready to emerge well-preserved,
   handsome
as that jogger on the boardwalk's burning PT slats.
It's not just re: fucking, but structural inequities
while attempting maintenance of finger snaps
some levity to wiggle with against the toxic
cousin of fatalism's gesture or void.

He slept in haze in a lean-to behind pylons
and was thus insulated, genre of irony
that fills a reverie of my lungs, pals
with the air of my fat morning.

Photographs which did not resemble
blurring; brace
the name of the lake
lodged in my liver,
a friend recalled eaten
by sand.

Say the conviction:
stained dark red
porch light on all night.

We are ultimately flimsy
hotdogs getcher hotdogs
foreclosed in that sense
stuck in the ravines
we constructed but unable to cry
or comprehend our lack of marrow,
how we once scooped it out of ourselves like little canoes
    in a wilderness
where to cry was lit and we were undressed.
My pouty lips made you sad and we were without clothes,
    laconic,
ready to strafe our notions of will in our birthday suits.
Birthmark on my inner thigh, a healthy ration
of scars inedible despite your tonguing
that makes for laughter. Shaking
my memory will waste its sweetness always
on misallocation of my senses rising
toward outer orbs and you, damned
like me in a bush wiping
sweat from neck down.

And yet it poured on our besmirched nitrile gloves,
rotund plastic bag contents spilt.
Then a rejected tea-time's oinking atmosphere,
his ass all cute but he's a bastard
and I'm a door slam blocks away,
remains of ascendance trapped on one of these split stoops,
cool and emeralds we
were told to hum, told to whistle until
we desired not we
buried in our mania for morning honk of juice
interning our synaptic prunings and blubbery yearning
in the hills.

The walls of black chalcedony
reflect a portent of my visage,
loose mesh attached to institutional pattern
color bands highway breakdown lane.

Sporting worsted trousers in a cenote
and a second dose of river light
in which I stare at a bum rousing on a steam vent.

Question: we did know how else to put it,
so we relaxed into gooey lyric,
can't spit, slick goo molars:
Is't the end?
An interrogative that concerns you and me because
   it continues to happen
in iterations. We dicked around the rhizome
and put up some posters, reach of a block or six,
American as opening the hydrant
'cuz we're in for this for
doused cotton against skin,
holding your breath in green anticipation
of more sensuousness, a power
against its writhing self.

Many blank unstaring hairstyles searing
the cursèd huge pupil factory
almost quaint now,
like we were riding through desert:
polite way to say
we were seeing nought but mayhem
in each other's viscera,

hurt by a national refuge,
arms and back scraped with pus
later in the hot tub's warfare compendium
and lovemaking, we gnawed on bones.
In fact, we gnawed on freezer-burnt metaphor
and called it bones flickering all the graves dug,

the guilt on the bluffs and the glopping sand later,
everything demolished but parking lot.

Has been a temporal hovering cradle I throw
confetti vernal and deep luxury therefore
odd perimeters of self-belief.
Speaking the most with a machete
under a bridge masturbating
and a guy pushing buttons that,
contrary to his drive home from base,
constitute the yolk of our epoch:
ennui of absence overtaken
by fondling hands in the hallway,
no war but all the particulates we breathe and thus,
citizens or no, there is a party
we're attending called SPLATTER
when we need a more inventive approach:
let's get to mixing cob, I'll thatch,
nice day to pretend, in fact, to appearances.

In search of a better salted cellulose flake, I
wish to sleep with the ghost in this ceiling
in the basement,
never heard that track before—
it's taking me for a swishing
the glass of the immediate.

Shadow wrestling heat once summer hits
from below and we all need dental work
was it fifteen years ago in a gold Aerostar,
and was there a stashed wad of bills
in heavy weeds pillaging asphalt?

Density of a speck of Chengdeite, this
eternal recurve shot
new life no life.

Rather it's what they eke, body like juice
consecrated in cellophane
doing trouble or a ditty and if I should falter
a living, a metaphor
for a wall, damn libretto
souping through my panties
as wage, or opening eyes
wide and ploughing through
"We'll never be this young again,"

so thresh labourers in abstruse skin slaps
a parody kissing abdomen vitamin lips
cheap tile, cheap in nearby brick kilns
pumping out what slurs,

epistemology that dances for money
boom boom or by the airport extended stay hotels
I huff euphemism for sport each night
like paps took long walks
and we only had one tub covered in cum
distilling moonshine.

You put in the video and there's a phantom
then crunching as the machine poofs out
animal trails of smoke,
repetitive pronoun weeping
confusedly over raw chicken flesh
focusing the mind on its hinterland:
stroking mold spores on a neighbor's stucco,
what do you recommend me?

I dithered with the slapping and unloading
the dirt thus we're fobbed with fayre wordes
and deconstructed boxes of rotting rutabaga.
And suicide week ended! Fuck! Gruelest decade
Polaroid exhibition, a nude blonde, seedy room,
"Once you put a deposit down we give
you the remote," grease on the screen
of the canon and a decommissioned foot bridge
over the cut, piece of honey in its place.

Any American suburb a mafia
of bait bags with motorways,
the oasis of anywheres
is the bloody chainsaw shower scene.

Hypersecurity system collapsed
resolution a cleanse play,
possible sightings threatened
to want someone,
rising sun.

The b-side is "Paranoid in the Sunlight."
It tracks like beach mutilation
gloomed bench cans sweat.
I ripped it as I could to disappear
figured out this shush like I'd tasted it
on a bit nail twenty years ago.

We ate hot sausages in a dark bar.
I sometimes picked up my book.
There was no real sequence it read
and we agreed, bushy on the roof holding
pebbles getting drummed opalescent
vest my envy sonnet on cornflakes
my envy to wind the clocks
and to forcefield.

I had no faith in what I had been:
two lengths of interpretation
connoting absorption and refusal
or despair for the anglerfish swimming the carpet.
Of an adjustable frame I balladeer! To cut
the smile and iron lung called sexual,
the dim parties of fish stix and pharaohs
rolling stock scoring a serenity not ribald,
but a family's sabbath diner trip, ergo
obscene blood gel and flapjacks with cut fruit,
laptop missing the "U" and "M" keys.

Dratty scanning the lots' yawn
right when it hits like copters
bollocksing their hover,
eagle and bobcat testicles on the roof
were these scenes I espied in an artichoke,
aperitif coinage, slink of an opal capital stolen,
that is, veiled and base.

Some might be called potentiators
seeping wetland crowding
into a shade
my unregiments,
dash of formulating thunderheads.
Suspicious thoughts for office,
reasons why cliffs seduce and more reasons
to abandon there smearing hell
patty muck between bread
in quotes coping well
intransigent follicle tickles the threat
as expectation and accessory
to skanky cameras held together
with packing tape
arresting us all.

I see that and raise you a van,
some trees, maggots, leaving the fire.

To plug and plug away as moistened witness
on secret malachite outcropping beyond resurgent
and rinsed cuffs mistaking a salad spinner
for the ontic of time and nibbling wildly,
exclaiming how into it you might be:
wobbling antenna, interrupted broadcast
fetish goes worldwide.

Thighs rubbing petals for a month at my place,
mush mush an enormity of our demands
versus argyria and whispers
that can't find explanatory notes
on mud's terrific fortress splatted in my brain.
I just see heaps of burning livestock if I dream.

Me damning this dumpsite's expanse of crabgrass,
funneling myself into an affect, rolling it
into large balls, smashing then broiling them.
I linger with impulse: month's muddy river inheritance
on my back, stick two fingers there and a fun riddle emerges
involving a lone desk's failure to travel beyond
its windswept furrow.

I sit and count the dances they call,
squeezing more and more discarded positions
into my hip-hugger's holsters weighed down
with recursive sentiment, sham intuition
like I died in a botched robbery
under a willow,
drool inflecting a dog mattress, oh daddy
brought treats so now I'm coated.

Throating my photocopied maps to liquidate pings,
the Spirit of Romance facing mortality in Provence
or Green River still crossing S at Uinta overpass for WBD,
your mind itching confusedly, thus my morning
stalk through sly corrosion, fermented at hose hook-up.

What I'm getting at is the surety back to those eons:
scratching ourselves on some resinous stumps
money on the camp stove's windbreak,
underoo grit at river bottom.

I find yes I find deep jollity in retroflection
kick me to the curb, de-ribbon my nog-nog
and spike me to what is always the literary present,
so that this cramped whinny shows I am attempting
forceful turning, asking where I slather,
where I shame myself, where can pollen suck at me denying
all my calls and other coupons.

An amalgam of glowing sounds
sanding my waning grammar
conatus lonely as smooshed daffodil intersection.
Mine drama: abandoned pallets across the stream
another's breath on the payphone
distanced-qua-accomplished-in-yellow,
dressed to drip torch the blood of Christ
or snake holes and ornery wooden masquerades
worshipping goo of justification all over these ropes
and of course the shack
loaded with bitch of sugar licky
and subtle desperado—they are inventor's shoes
found miles from the car.
We followed them in but strayed from the speaker.

Afar, the epic duck plumage skitters the breeze,
burns off my rusts and my deformity,
destined to identification with the shabbier and lateral
weather patterns running wet finger
crystal rim glittering from the state.

Sultry and gobble unofficial food pantry
hauling association and when they did find her
she was in the valley in need.

As structure looks but spine knife physical comedy
and visceral curvature, forked thus less solid
up the hill with diesel and glacier mire flexing,
middle of renovation truck stop.

Looking proximal to ratty Snoopy slippers,
my zone is wire and wandering key in hand
through chronicles of false doors, theory
with its ombré and insistence
right on the village green.
Scenic accents were wooks and casualties
sucker-punched in grime at low tide.

Rhythm and abandon
storms in spring.
Lewd whispers and warnings
some gates
on the road.

Persistent secret
awes me and heavily
fills me,
various papers scattered around.

Build an interpreter for this lulling croon
massage ramps and beam
casing sausages of these other brick walls
what amount to silence and performance.

They do yearn for it, plot of screen
segmented insolence and recovery
to beans, rice, like we should absolutely not
slip on distracted tender grace but run
scars on each tit we view.

Affect of parking spot as swift analog
for Crisp Flippy the diplomat.
I burnt glut, dug into these hills and invested
in submarines, risky I know,
but never not wet oh.

Loose in the pattern's alarming confirmation,
I omit sense and begin again socked in poison and foment,
buckets behind the mini-mart as air-quote liberty,
sources of paralysis as proper response.

A demand for softer material in car boots
as salvo against rapture as construed
preferring a looping gif of a cigarette in a window's ashtray,
make a sashay of your subject and its house
while I suck on this bottle and its banishment
from figures approaching in damp smoke.

What change means to me, a distracted mite in a puddle
on a foothill, water as primary measure of skull fragments.
No ease of image. No farm observed
nor an repugnant moon or drying stones
but a shirking grey and a dense silo
brittling toward suspicion.

Distance forms the toxin of grief,
a temporal process and more equivalences
simpering near the microwaved popcorn batter
before the lights dim.

Your dick resembles his
sordid unlikely timeline,
bone-dry possible despair reprieve
flipping through anecdotes of revolt
and morning's visible breath
gesturing toward years curdled on tile,
sweat on public computer.
The foisted spleen rhyming
stains interrupting patter, hair, and blood
into the sill, poised dumb
and exactly like the novel read.

Causing the tight black leather glove to unclench
dropping blue motes to fold into
impressionable viscomte of the shallows
with his birthdays stacking to run the planet's rotation.

Emotional drydock perforce rubble in my shoulder
fiddling on my throat as I secrete onto this installation,
a rolled date in times of difficulty
these projections like her bathhouse babble,
as if what appeared could pay full fare.

They tried me with their books and I wept
and returned sleeping on a picnic table,
some naive composition, carpeted walls.

Cocktail in styrofoam and tulips on the promenade,
I face a trial but the bridge had been replaced
so my tendency toward kissy really blade
there on the stub's blankness under highway felching
sweetly it neighed in anticipation that
this is a sound stage
slick in a pinafore
concocted fessing in the holly grove:
a really, really inadequate eco-poem
developing then lunch in the ditch facsimile.

State office park the wind tonight,
charity milk dangerous revel soil nude
occult ceremony robe fitting.

I have also received a letter from a retired grazier
yet cannot whistle this melody,
or is it repulsive in its pinching physical promise
torrential and in cold doing wipe
festooned with ribbons I will imitate the voice
and dance with someone younger, blushing
at my scrimped resolution, her soapy areola
hand balances a screwdriver, tuneless but bouncy
mine dollop of chemicals as ivy fastens northward
to us babes in the attic, foreground in sacks.

These angels I consider: of rumor, of potential buff,
of a used pair of platform sneakers, of an image
of a silhouette burnt into a wall.

Sneaking up behind them I prepare my scissors
so that the issue becomes my boots
in blood and wing dross disdain all purpose,
a sad a sad a sad a sad called a natural threat
keeps rousting me from my spot on the floor's
empty binge set-piece.

According to the man who fakes his death,
struggling failed,
a form of transit burned,
in bad odor he assured
with his predatory demeanor
the available reward.

That he faces daily torment for his creation is good.
Glower at crinoline bows and water's evaporating bobbin
laws of laws a roving descant.
Start a new career in side highway dandelions
an impressionistic watercolor of a Frostie on the necktie
a sequence of events that moves through spirit becoming
the third winning ticket the small woman
had recently purchased.

Do not French my cynic's gut tapestry,
demanded new life and found it gnawing
so broke bread at every corner's blazing barrels.
Theory is fabulous remains of the salvage yard for incisors
uneven in its approximation of the form
it wished to chatter.

Humans with a trickle of blood
syruping from under their caps,
and humans scourged into fanciful networks
of claims skinnying out sense, getting pied
constantly an alley and a knife as metaphor
or sites so particular their narratives
are obscured.

Have a park at night with destroyed bus shelter
circulate the sequence of fagging
for symbolic necessity
for a decent fisting soundtrack
because gooshy and rising
from the dead four times
as so many have bred a bleak skepticism
in the audience forced to wash like animals.

Known otherwise as worn mattress on floor,
the frugality of the systematization seemed obvious
but sometimes danced well enough to ply
those cruising the watering holes as they closed.

The roots there, in his satchel, thrown
from a cliffside and splatting the beach below,
were unusable. Yea, the backpack curried no favor
with the long drive through the arbor.

Enough stories! I've this dismantled rifle
and imagination beyond plateaux— let's hurl
useless key collections at the concept of children,
to be on display as assured, frigid
snowbound hamster goals, that is tiny
teeth's rapid clicks in your sleep,
carrying a fondue set, a dainty dunk
into stupor's warmth.

The drive-in sucks—
people aren't a screen to glance at after
mollifying buds with sweeties or post-salival.
Confetti the world so bothersome,
so political the threshing yet demand flips
'til golden brown on both sides, crammed
nearly into the stomach with genital confidence.

I drank the tea, thus the cup
bottom strapped ruminates in welted cruelty,
not that there had to be gentler syllables:
driving across the state line for fireworks,
fancy tango violence in a really lovely part of the park
waggled its tail as we died screwed
to our phalanges with hundreds of urethral satellites
prancing in the altered field,
the staring contest wail emporium.

Had we more to scoff at? Taking all meals in bed
thus beginning life anew with strength, grace, and wonder
sardined by little scraps of prophecy
by rigid depths comprising the hounds' wooflings,
wistful sweat above the lips and the rocker
that finds itself stilling.

Fresh grass shanty constructed entirely of delusion
or worse, sand forcing open the jaw.
Whenever overtaken, I blame half-empty
electric in the mist embankment dreamy eye
pathology become a dirigible,
ovalling available sky.
She had never heard this no vacancy,
seething while clapping.

From a humid spectacle that strained narrativity,
a dewy face responds with a fork of neon,
a list of opposites that is the cuticle
of inveterate islanding, somber door dagging
in circles, brush on ride in an ampoule drip.
Sincere sauces distributing these chemicals
scarce, even more in this occasional punctuation,
the O horizon odour as mimeo found in a pile
next cycle, it is how we dowse then fix the air
into our froggy scandal, the dueling sputter
of our chances in DVDs permeates
the corner in that earlier chorale.

Came with plainness of interior fetishized,
extraordinary ripeness of reflection
confiscating armada of light
and jukebox crackle. The sorrow
that sorrow's already been there, that want
want lonely God was last year, this year's
kinetics more flexed and frayed—
icepick they say
machetes they say
stowing ourselves and another afternoon against the chest.

One day we'll tickle again, but cold gin,
automatic rifles, discerning smiles
beneath masks, my binky.

On the morning of
and outside of it,
they are dancing
this claim leaking
into the stream.

Trustworthiness attendant
to the company of an unknown man,
concrete banks disorient.

All this will count for little
newly admitted surrounding,
the ordinary vigil
waiting in the check out line.

Dog Day Scrolls

scratch
my scalp for me please, energy and revulsion
in which every living thing was an aberration
of itself
—Norma Cole, "Rosetta"

I. DOG

To Get Even More Cum

Greetings to the aerosol
of my dread composition
porous yet inward

use me quiet, use me
brackish   on a film paddled
deep ingestion of an epoch
better left sorry though not

sans charm, less predictive
and more prone watching the girls
cluck about the yard.

Our neighbors would shoot them
and laugh at our shovels, feathers
picked up by wind in search.

Daisy-Chained Ghost

A romance of snipers
langue wading in goo
please refrain from gendering
this being a stick-up, sweet thing,
licked abyssal image
feeling, my new dress
running my hands over
absorption levels,
the last fang
bullets
harmonizing
whistles
scales.

Our Dead Roses

Blew smoke through the hole
the rectangle provided
shocking in preceptual odor
unsmelled—simultaneous recurrence

I got it in me
stroked its sum
huffed paint from a bag

sat in my boil collection tray
called afternoon
this month
walking slowly through chlorinated water
your neck in my thumbs
fallibly moving upward in register
head in my hand bus shelter.

Inside My Magma

Up in the rafters
knocking in the room adjacent
shadowing the wall how you stare
staring at the wall's strategy
suggested as cultural emblem
there in the gutter
what amounts to dynamism
squeezing dough in my role
positioned 90 degrees
from any island siren
inside my magma
bent at tribunal
a series regarding posture
elevated toward your nipple
mouthing wildly never
never resound again.

Do People Stay Punk

When you shave
in a ritual
this or that
refuse following you.

Salad Shouts

I studied sorghum and shedding
            myself in the kitchen
                        by the butter rolls

nudity & public access
TV in the mid-to-late 1990s
bottled tears enjambed
to commitment, oddest syndication
those wispy swollen years in abeyance.

Dread's formality uploads me
as I waltz into an unfamiliar honky-tonk.

Banned and Good

Damned to salvage,
explicate the tune she's humming,
mine to misplace, admit
how often I jerk it in the cell,
corpse at desk, cold pallet,
stiffening
in grace of delusion.

Terrible countenance
being offered a bukkake scene,
repression's fingers lollying
my interstitial spaces
shaved unevenly.

Stands in the blue
in the foreground
the world is banned
and good, shallow
wet in night's dark yard.

Spake Sodden

Give me the swimming pool
of each swallow
made over a lifetime
of singing Jack & Jill
your finger in the morning
in exultation shake it
alone you're all right California
didn't step outside
dippin' down
genitally comfortable
in an mini-mart bathroom
video video video video video

Number and Name

Making water at Target
place of eels of scalps
on hold as a bird
listens in we are sorry
for the weight.
                Painted-on jeans
ain't it but close to clicking
it all ceases I went out
from myself declaratory in lilacs
public sculptures vague graceful.

Always this excitation
first volleys of what's coming—
denied dread I whisper in hoops
obscenity obscenity obscenity
dying less fast today, perhaps
exposed ribs frequency.

The Oranges

When curtains
billow inward
Flesh and argument
re: flesh discontinued

In the light juggling
two pairs of undies
and a bar
or two, hum that one
goes a tree
planted by the water.

Knew About the Ass

Universe as set of stairs:
to us a child is born.

Neon of tooth and seers
hair in fist in chorus
they were on K2 when
the sandbags failed.

Time's rake   *"just a pinch"*
tubes sanguine above hip
unsure of this bowl of bile
imprecision, helpless laughter.

Your Bussy Would Get So Tired

Calque or troubled urn
providing boundary, womb,
"Git yrself some 41147s
at the Harbor Freight,
we'll reconnoiter here in an hour,"

baked stringy, yep,
caught in a scam crossing myself
then singing empties round a curve,
ate the cans, nodded out
in the pile of blood
forbidding sleep addressed to dim
concepts French dipping logic
dignifying romance in this refrigerator box
with a blowie that woke up the pooches.

Biological Material

I stay exulting in circular solitude,
my buttocks milk-crate world
                                        mettle like a slab
of beef and gin's tourist
city recalls the spongy aspects
of the mouth, darling
sacrifice here, belt a round out

absorb what's through the firs
I sin never again I glance
at my erection
the valley low
the drought the back of his neck.

Hawthorne Spritzer

In the afternoon flesh
smacking each step—

whine opening crisp missives
faggotry of thumb riding
true in the treacle mawkish
under sable skies

to each a leprachaun voice, confusion,
life as a hovering spatula
no better strategic implementation
than the rack we all deserve,

technicolor 80's peepholes
eggs eggs eggs forehead—
another galaxy? Gross.

II. DAY

The Hi-Way Gown

Watched it struck
by front unit flown
on ballast the sound of which

how do I begin
to discipline my egos past
shirtless in a shovel drunk

et for dinner
fudge, later bushwhacking,
resign in hurry
puke Zingers in brush
topple as in urine in yr jeans out cold
chippies at your back
singed pubes on stove
dependency my morning chuckle.

Central Soup

At a gallop my ankle buckled
all fates aligned in this way
metaphor another dark star
damp in my greetings

       about the sorry neigh
or cliffside's pacific retrenchment

sorry to dust in his hair
notes bent in mahogany

gorgeous sticky
cowbells across the fields

unremarkably shadows
wither compass.

Dismissed Array

Sly thunder we force on
sultry in the funnel scrawled
developing strategies for decades

clothes muddy on shore envelop
sight's calamity,
thespian of muck, sorry
dithering in silt's nomos

gulf between the reflecting
flaws crossing eastward.

Ellipsis as Phantasm

Churning angle of jay's neck
sours my beneficence
fake shutter snaps
months of notifications
pretty roiled
creek garbage
big salad dog notes
caved-in grave walls
slender, tethered
to a most plastic source
awoo-ing in a station wagon
pumped dry unfilled
forms gesturing toward a mirror
or mirrors curbed fragrance
ellipsis as phantasm I see myself
a decade on.

With Holes

Shingled in pablum
yet taller far
cheeks bulged
with absence,

gong's painstaking appeal to time
rewrite everything thus the slum
of my attempts,
tinkling cymbal simulation
guttural, pitiable across star system.

I positioned my body offensively,
applauded breeze with ears cottoned
in attention as fondness, yes,

you were saying about

yes, the myth of God in spite
of my feeling for this light
ferrying the most skyward branches
toward donuts with holes,
a test site in garden
shrub unwanted but beloved
skeletal emergency and childish prank.

'Chemical Oats'

A good time person
as regression, twirling my tool
in the fucks of famine
desert me
misplaced emphasis
yackety no facile muscle car
an occulted township where I strip,
finicky impersonating cruelly.

Dust muffling pores
two dollar buds whinging on shore
damask grit in teeth
flagellating cedar dew
and dumpy fragrant hills
a being rolled.

Verdant Mimic

Which stupefied them:
decadent evidence
slatternly birdsong
limber-limp but punchy above
a haunted water trap.

Shouts from fuselage
guarantee no fair quiet
and fine, slick.
That's you,
unable to extract yrself
from floating
fish as staffage pinching,
robotic voice uttering 'Arcadia.'

Under the Jumbotron

As it glistens on the hands

Ember in wind
    (enough in hole)
        spatial patterns
   judged without verbs
    barracks vision
  exceptional murder corral
valley curve at summit

Painful access
or dormancy rhyming with self
dark tunnel beyond where rests
lasso, short lecture on the diminished sixth
a juicy grape that's skin plumped
at the tonsils playing possum
      luggage packed then tossed
in the reservoir
philosophy was wrong.

Scrawled w/ Chapstick

My odor remains so
let's shake on it
sole computer in the commune jacked
by malware, a distinct yellow banging
against press-on shower tile.

Clouds signal ruin
and figures sloughing up a hill
playing to an ill-maintained
smiling in the boiler room.

Walkable Village

We repose on a skull that's the bit
scale model located inside th'original

flash flood I spiral

into a dropped ice cream
think of the sidewalk's feelings
slick with grime in love
with itself and your ass
scooching its mouth glad
to feel similarly in sun.

Shoulder Over

If you view the hammer caught
in the intersection as enemy-cum-
hissing-goose, delete that ferment
from your replicator. Yes,
hug the claw chewing
through shore's glass,
pecking at referents like this groove,
like there glowed a green spectre
in reeds, mighty tight
shoulder over diaper creek
but also ineffable arc slants
in the melody packin' up its plans
after a day's doze.

Dopey Undercommons

Sense overrated and I cross into puddles
breathing ruined garments.

Another word for resent, a Powerpoint: Husqvarna,
bone, efficiency charts for chest freezers, queasy on
descent, dapper and sweating,
degraded sun worship making muscles
dark corner of the subgenre severed head.

Save presentation.

Disused memorial garden library
spiritualist guide M
is for pulp high
pomo sincerity up a tree
lesson down
crumbs in window
locks on doors
bathetic and famished.

See Freeway, See Flames

To think, to be hardly bipedal
turning to cubbies, hedges
diggin' warm spray in home front doubtless gutter
doubtless we're mostly in trenches

breathing as chaff welcoming
rats to steal
at our
meat center waiting area.

Houdini's Anger

Filled with unmixed fire
we head to leech our tannins
parking lot's northeast corner
approximate location of jadeite chorus
aka irreparable harm barbecue
outside his pterodactyl shed.

Gonna be with you:
chair swinging at skull
exists inside all time,
hence its ambience
speed stash hollow cinderblock.

Illusions persuasive and tangy
                    take a bite
then let's rob someone,

just a sip
getting better every year.

Right on Target

Never danced without a war
bouncing bosom probed by finger
flexible edge of intent
talking into a can
to passed iterations

whaddaya mean frame of
slammed down bag
eyes' westward gaze
skin and dirt that is your skin balled
between index finger and thumb
without a pleasing sound.

Wake Up Sheeple

Let me pilfer
with more about that whistle
breathy adjacent CBD.
Could a blade be reduced thus
crackling in a town sub sub
interrupted series
thus a trough where we gut

a lake of decision
kippered or smoked teen lust
                    fingers in honey
don't bustle me
'cause I'm a bad puddle
never fostered an east never
thought about crime.

Sadie and the Virtuous

i.
Holding hands with the extravagant line
between last seen and body found
is desirous parcel aerating,
here referring to my block party
beside myself at car trunk,
dripping my wee cells a dance
with many falls to name.

ii.
Thighs on suede, your nipple when
we first met, shirk of actuality
            refuge overlooking basin
horseshoes peeling off skeleton

cruelty's idiot also collects
water from the stream shoving
into cataract, lost camp
satchel in the threads pulling.

A Broken Trumpet

or lash myself
to a puke with sprinkles
beheaded and gathering mold
yell's long shade I walk in
tiled view reaper variation.

Samba of constant grief
arms with feathered long gloves
and intentional lack of squirrel suit—

the clown was dropped
from a helicoptor
into the ocean and there erupted
hail of recognition,
trawling waves for our dispersal,
arrogance of assuming shore louder
than the engine seizing.

Dorsal Cynicism

Slammed it in the door
too busy humming ""Funkytown"
           the scythe   language
as taproot, as glooming flats,
views from the state's tallest building.

Strategy emergent
my waters

Deutch of innuendo overfeed outmode
           a torso covered in licorice
mowing innocuous phrases in the field:
"breath fester"   "dorsal cynicism"
lovingly braving my facial tics
bound and schooled

                     creosote and the
                       you recall

The Hermitage

Where summit lurks
so does foretype
bruising apple flecks
sand down my box.

Weary of garden, of boulder,
stripers watery & featureless
I crave that element dangling
in horizon

unremembered that sensate vessel
that solo on the rocks below
comparison then doubt, as ever
pocked bleat erupting the throat.

Gated

Cannot be avoided
bend back   pelvis forward
oh chirping   oh rashes

Demand fealty to presence
what follows bellows
growls silky crown west

Last century's thick glass fragments

I said, "Gulp," I said, "moron," I said
"my" in a divot
smacked the rotting unbothered hum
a song, dear that dalliance

ten feet up thick first
slight diagonal keloid
diagonal in a baggage claim
another's hand inner thigh
so rough slender plasticine

Pilgrim Creek Antique Mall

Stock image van under trees
desire's simple thus:
to forfeit scrum deliquesce at the ghost
declaring itself ocean or otherwise

just below treeline
we bicycle fifteen miles
each way to town
once per week share a smoke
on the drag's sallow damage.

New tarp, matches, bushels wax
beans and buckwheat our backs
uphill toward camp's batteries drained.

Never get sick, never eat the berries
labradorite in my pocket
what breathes on us each evening.

Buford Special

Not even marginalia
not a mote thus trapped
we spent the day on speed
attempting the horse body
in rain, delicatessen floor,
translated comment you sing
along to like flies
down the pit latrine
I touch the remains
of my taint thinking
that's harmony's pleasure, dumbo.

Moustache Against

Sidling up to the sump pump
Namibian beach porn to say
ever at fisticuffs with the glowing
quartzite brained there
morning then surfaces on tape delay
growth overtaking clearcut
dastardly waveform, horrible
angel cheeks

Yea, no valley no peace
soft moustache against the wall
sugar in his tank recursion
or youthful loogie at void
those who wear it like comfy jammies

unable to sleep
unable eyelids
to laugh again
echoing into static.

The Huguenots

And in our sourceness
and in our simple parade
        distrusted thought

glasses thick with red slurry
leaving approximately round reminders on structure
        styrofoam's resonant frequency, too

puncturing lifeline digging space
for celosia to go Yoko
wailing through theft knighted
        futile diversion   revolting web of
skin
        revolting sadism of the warnings

We drink and I step on the porch
sway in what can only be described
as fanged declension
irrational in field, french friend
        genitalia commercial, lushness
        of our necks in scope.

III. SCROLLS

Unplaced Hayride

notorious illumination

felony myth of felony

counting each rib

the coldest glass of water

tides of pleasure at next window

detasseling sensibility

hillock and colt

carcass as season for

tending to the snag's nuthatches

deep in pulp

fastened to the glottal of revulsion

Hibachi of the Conscience

The moat between my feelings
and an ethics is
an anti-convulsant
I slowly drip down
my own leg, fool reservoir,
walls blanched and indeterminate,

own boulder knocking
down from its heights
approaching my flesh impediment,
fingered yet splashy
hibachi of the conscience,
a stripmall in Dayton.

Live Facedown

Feed this Funnydew melon
I found in an Ohio
geocache in '06
to our friend over there.

We all agree we are into butter
in suspension, whirling fat
as jadrools gleaning

all the following
belong to the bastard.

Wrong Pustule

How the chords are played

stupor on the rocks

at the national kiosk

fitting a gym-sock over

all things are full

boarded up well

prying as paradigm

as glass jutting slipper

tsuris dressed in skintight lycra

what is morning scree

drainage from the burn where we touched

passed around some Brut

splashing evidence encasing itself

monad whimpering

as I flip over the mattress

A Knobby

Delivery refused
clafouti of my harbinger,
succulent herbs haptic at window.
Dare I falsify my homework,
stride up to the hangar
jingling my keys
and a Manwich reveal
at my mouth's corners.

They laughed at us
in the courtyard,
cum in our hair.
They's dead or chemtrails
that's what's sprayed,
think of your dead
wonder jet beyond so many.

"Push Me to the Edge"

Supped on rain
ringing and fugue at longer intervals,
        each interminable
swiping summer puffy

        I do not give myself
        shade as in space
        enclosed and
                without flips

        Counting the contoured pools
where sweat collects on yr face
erupts airport-adjacent government office cul-de-sacs
fumbling for a light
birdbath in gas station
we ate berries

                Our cruel soliloquies cassette turning
        over again, lips wet on a Golden Deer.

I'm talking to you, Cherry Face,
purple rug
a bag of skins
a bottle.

Adult Bungalow

Of the soul the frosted tips
deny stroke alas the suite
held together by nowhere accent.

Large teenage obvious
at the pool
greasy chemical tile
shrieking underwater shot
sure slalom around requisition
that frustrates me.

I want
        shrugging
I think of you every bridge.

Supine Tally

i.
Held like stars
   thus immovable knee-deep
in an eddy's moon
        and buxom
with lists of disavowals.

ii.
Pickin' at the sutures
bloody flan hotdog
remember you   a funny yellow wash
on the ultrasound, two curtains
patterns two can play
the gospel   blasts
             safe

the game flake an unforgiven
detour and rest,
        cursed,

I wanted boogie but these knots dripping.

Not Digging the Chancellor

Rag or day itself

                    force of a stone

that appears at vacuum's center
that video you filmed of the valley floor

somber there
and fleck
of spit
corner of mouth
washing down
in threshold to
juicy

Humping Twins

in pixellated lament
in foaming wave recession
the bedstraw outlasts us
sartorial equivalent a hocked
cresting phlegm unnoticed, grey
drawstring sweatpants build out
late in the song sense
of evening's usual pangs
dilated sakes of mangling.

Twilight a Century Ago

Lost in standard pinprick beads
arranged like brunch
in a pup tent

twilight a century ago

What's absent that snarls
query about your recent order.
Knees dipping against the beat
we ended up at, saying

bow bow bow bow glass
coated in pills hung sloppy
on the landing a squall,
a sanitized preen monument

swells as it renders.
Lucky tidal memory,
balms and whalers.

Gruel Blast

As the blob blossoms 'round
a poplar balsam aflame,
ladling continues in each tin cup,
mouthing grubs and ferns
as the stories promised.

Bandits of consequence sap
a sirloin of imaginal north
that's to shuck unpronounceable
some other illusions. My birth
a shoddy linearity
your cheeks dormant in a smack.

We tested the cabin
waves recklessness kindling
reworked hum's sticky response
to where we summoned pages and where
we forced out all we can.

User-Created Weather Impressions

Tuck a couple scotch eggs
into the respirator,
drive to the long tail,
demand yr snowbank shape up
into a snickering ice hotel.

Clinky-clinky designer past
shirtless drugs a deathless pool,
enamored of begging holes
depthless in their context,
crimsoned dearth like
warm fluid collecting
running predictably shabby
in curs of another season.

Sunken Vesicle

Forgot to wash the bits of bone out

        bluff overlooking pasture's interstate

    episode in a Subway truckstop
    recursion of force as theme
    came in with famine drawn
    fever in granary reddened fingertips
    palaver as treeline
        obscuring the pits.

Oversized Antenna

The performance of education
as a logic also on stage
playing two notes dressed
in tatty garble when naked
would be less seductive
grunting
praise in crackling speakers
at the far river

wounded while noodling
ready fallacy of the leather
coated in dirt coats me

"Naturally Motionless"

the drawers after two weeks
are again clean
raring for the unlimited
moments encasing genitalia parades
its excretions clear
in this climate
more like wheeze than usual.

Anytime Plaything

Tossing the invisible ball around
in our lack of comprehension
what panting amounts to
floodwater dildo touching tree
of heaven's voice carrying me
on its shoulders kicking,
"YOU ARE NOT PARADISE!"

Dangling an oblique rime,
grimace in biting the lyres
drawn like air trending toward
clarity of droplets there,
further glint and fractal.

The Mission (2012)

One cumulonimbus says to another,
"I never flirted so pathetically,"
light drizzle collections
rot in cotton lining
crosstown afternoon
books in waistband
purloined soil experiment.

Sordid glove will show them.

Theory: it's a j-cat tent
to muttering glow
closing in and off ramp.

Caged in Lace

A living sorbet in chunks
deeply aligned hot borg hour
in depths of drink
leaves resembling glue
daffy tunnel à la Susan
modulation facility
and the poodle's ennui.

Horse Tongue

Deleting my messages from this forum
to find the crest in all pulp
and reside there, flat cars
chug north dirty
conveyance so potent
we peek into its coffin.

One big second
line without space distortion
cradling my corneas' smush so
many things we recall sleeping
over a tub of cream
left for the ponies to lick
jagged forehead scar
guilt that lives
there in the face.

Notes on the Poems

The poems of *Economy, A Reshaped Spit* were composed by writing with and around language that was physically cut and pasted from issues of *The Economist* magazine and Wikipedia articles on people who have disappeared mysteriously, with special attention given to those who seem to have disappeared voluntarily. They were written in Philadelphia between November 2019 and May 2020.

The poems of *Dog Day Scrolls* were first composed on large sheets of butcher paper utilizing luggage markers, permanent markers, packing tape, scraps of paper, and pens, in a rather physical process. They were written in Philadelphia between 2020's summer solstice and autumnal equinox.

Acknowledgements

Previous versions of some poems appeared in *A Perfect Vacuum, bæst: a journal of queer forms & affects, KEITH LLC,* and *Nomaterialism.* Thanks to Judah Rubin, Noah Ross, Zan de Parry, and Carlos Lara for giving them their first homes.

I value having been given the opportunity to speak some of these poems at readings for the Segue Reading Series, Woodland Pattern, and AN INSIDE. Thanks to curators Lonely Christopher, Venn Daniel, the Woodland Pattern crew, and Lewis Freedman.

Stacy Szymaszek took a first gander at *Economy, A Reshaped Spit* and gave some valuable feedback, for which I am forever grateful.

None of these poems could have been written without the valuable support and feedback of many wonderful friends, especially Mark Johnson, J. Gordon Faylor, Danielle LaFrance, and Ariel Resnikoff. Your belief in these poems means a great deal.

I'd also like to thank dear friends Jessa Farkas, Jordan Mitchell, Oki Sogumi, Adam Kaplan, Jason and Marta Mitchell, Leo Famulari, Allison Chomet, Sarah DeGiorgis, Levi Bentley, Christy Davids, Jim Krull, Brittany Taylor, Ami Dang, Joey De Jesus, Sasha Mandel, Sydney Tanigawa, Joshua Castaño, Kyle Chvasta, Lucinda Trask, Lawrence Giffin, John Rufo, Jasmine Gibson, Ian Dreiblatt, Anna Gurton-Wachter, Jeremy Hoevenaar, Thom Donovan, Erin Morrill, Laurence Jones, and Eric Sneathen, among too many others to name. Your presence in my life, from near and far, made existence bearable enough to write these books.

I am ever thankful and humbled by the words of Robert Glück, Jennifer Soong, and Clint Burnham. Thank you for taking the time to read and remark upon these strange books.

Ted Rees is a poet, essayist, and editor who lives and works in Philadelphia. His most recent book of poetry, *Thanksgiving: a Poem*, was a finalist for a 2021 Lambda Literary Award. His first book was *In Brazen Fontanelle Aflame* and chapbooks include *the soft abyss*, *The New Anchorage*, and *Outlaws Drift in Every Vehicle of Thought*. He is the founder and co-editor of Asterion Projects, and editor-at-large for The Elephants.